Rain on the Pacific Coast

☙

by

Elbert Siu Ping Lee

RAIN ON THE PACIFIC COAST is a tapestry of human experience, in which desires and passing worlds crisscross, collude, and collide. Each poem is a tiny spark that flies off in various types of encounter, giving significance and illumination to seemingly brief and mundane moments of daily existence. The poems are rooted in space and time and involve real people. Read in a certain way, they are mini life-dramas. Behind the scenes, the poet plays the roles of provocateur, critic, voyeur, seducer, lamenter, lover, and spiritual guide. Many of the poems were written in different places in Hong Kong around the time of change over. Others were conceived at various locations from Eastern Canada to the Pearl River Delta.

ELBERT LEE was raised in Hong Kong and has studied in Hong Kong, Canada and New Zealand. His poems have appeared in a number of magazines and e-journals, including *Cha, Fusion, Muse Magazine*, and *Poetry Macao*. He has also contributed poems to a number of anthologies, namely, *Fifty/Fifty: A New Anthology of Hong Kong Writing* and *Hong Kong Poems: an English German Anthology*. His reading interests range from cognitive science, evolutionary biology, to Taoism and Buddhism. A member of the adjunct faculty of Upper Iowa University, he teaches psychology at the Hong Kong Campus. Elbert studied at McGill University, the University of Hong Kong, and the University of Auckland, where he obtained his Ph.D. in Psychology. He is currently involved in designing teaching materials for students.

Supported by

The Hong Kong Arts Development Council fully supports freedom of artistic expression. The views and opinions expressed in this project do not represent the stand of the Council.

Rain on the Pacific Coast

ෆ

by

Elbert Siu Ping Lee

Proverse Hong Kong

Rain on the Pacific Coast
by Elbert Siu Ping Lee.
Published in a different format, August 2016
ISBN: 978-988-8228-58-4
Copyright © Proverse Hong Kong, August 2016.
Available from https://www.createspace.com/6412747.

1st published in Hong Kong by Proverse Hong Kong, November 2013.
Copyright © Proverse Hong Kong, November 2013.
ISBN 978-988-8167-39-5

Enquiries: Proverse Hong Kong, P. O. Box 259, Tung Chung Post Office,
Tung Chung, Lantau Island, NT, Hong Kong SAR, China.
E-mail: proverse@netvigator.com Web site: www.proversepublishing.com

The right of Elbert Siu Ping Lee to be identified as the author of this work
has been asserted by him
in accordance with the Copyright, Designs and Patents Act 1988.

Cover design by Elbert Siu Ping Lee and Artist Hong Kong Company.
Page design by Elbert Siu Ping Lee.

All rights reserved. No part of this publication may be reproduced, stored in a retrieval system, or transmitted, in any form or by any means, electronic, mechanical, photocopying, recording or otherwise, without the prior written permission of the publisher or publisher and author. The book is sold subject to the condition that it shall not, by way of trade or otherwise, be lent, re-sold, hired out or otherwise circulated without the author's prior written consent in any form of binding or cover other than that in which it is published and without a similar condition including this condition being imposed on the subsequent owner or purchaser.
Please contact Proverse Hong Kong (acting as agent for the author) in writing, to request any and all permissions (including but not restricted to republishing, inclusion in anthologies, translation, reading, performance and use as set pieces in examinations and festivals).

**British Library Cataloguing in Publication Data.
A catalogue record for the first edition of this book is available from the British Library.**

Prior Publication Acknowledgements

'The Great Wah Fu Public Housing Estate' and 'City Chant' first appeared in *Fifty/Fifty: A new anthology of Hong Kong Writing*. Ed. Xu Xi. Haven Books, Hong Kong, 2008.

'Bamboo Grove', 'Blood Amber', 'In the Great City', 'Moments', 'Night Poems', 'The State of My House' and 'Where Would I Be' were first published, with German translations, in *Hong Kong Poems: an English-German Anthology*. Eds, Louise Ho, Klaus Stierstorfer, Monika Gomille. Stauffenburg. Tübingen, 2006.

'Masseuse from Shenzhen', 'Bo Bo of Wu Han' and 'Tai Tai Bodhisattva' were published in, *Poetry Macao September 2008*. Ed Christopher Kelen.
http://poetrymacao.comuf.com/PM_issue2/main.htm

'Ginger Flower Woman' was first published in *Asian Cha*, Issue 2, November, 2007. Ed. Tammy Ho Lai Ming.
http://www.asiancha.com/index.php?option=com_content&task=view&id=72&Itemid=88

'Masseuse in Shenzhen', 'Tai Tai Bodhisattva' and 'D'Aguilar Street' were first published, with Chinese translations, in *Muse Magazine*, Issue 1, September 2006, Ed. Perry Lam. Muse Magazine Publishing Limited, 2006.

'You Can Stay on this Ferry Forever', *Fusion*, No. 6, Prairie Schooner (stories, poems, essays and reviews since 1926), USA, published in cooperation with the University of Nebraska Press and the Creative Writing Program of the University of Nebraska-Lincoln English Department, online, http://prairieschooner.unl.edu/?q=fusion/water

Foreword

A few years ago, I had the pleasure of interviewing Elbert Lee for a project on contemporary Asian poetry in English. Lee wrote his first poem in New Zealand, on the other side of the Pacific Coast, as a mature adult:

> I was involved with ... a monastic group ... And we ... created ... a newsletter for the religious community ... There was a place in New Zealand, the North Island. In the middle of the island, there is an extinct volcano ... It was very beautiful. ... There was very thick moss, very colourful moss. It belonged to us. The whole trip prompted me to think about the imagery, to write something about the mountain, the volcano. ... not just because of the beauty, but also the ecological implications ...

The inspiration Lee felt in that spiritual community gathering on an otherworldly mountain prompted him to write. Since returning to Hong Kong, Lee has continued to be inspired by places and people around him. Although he also enjoyed writing essays and short stories, he confessed, "poetry ... can express something ... deeper, ... a view of myself or the world ... It represents my personal being more than stories."

Some of Lee's early works appeared in the 2006 English-German anthology of Hong Kong poems edited by Louise Ho, Klaus Stierstorfer and Monika Gomille, published by Stauffenburg in Tubingen, Germany. Lee has been very much a member of the Hong Kong poetic community. A festive poetry reading he organized on Peng Chau, the offshore island of his home, attracted several poets from the community and about 2,000 visitors. He is also represented in the on-line *Fusion* issue on Hong Kong to be published in August 2013 by Prairie Schooner in the United States of America. The community Lee writes to is very diverse – from the very local to the very universal and this is reflected in his poetry.

Rain on the Pacific Coast is a rich culmination of his work over the years. One recognizes readily the portraits of life or lives in Hong Kong presented with authenticity and empathy. Lee does not shy away from the more external prosperous images of Hong Kong as captured in 'Good Morning IFC' built literally with brand names around the world. Yet, at the same time, he can capture the pathos of the women devotees of such an affluent lifestyle, as in 'Tai Tai Bodhisattva':

> This is the routine you go through
> from day to day –
> casting beautiful reflections
> on shop floors and glass displays.
> This is your work, this is your faith.
>
> I keep my silence as I meditate
> from place to place
> casting doubt on the proceeds
> of your day.
> This is my work, this is my way.

In direct contrast is the mode of existence of those who try to survive 'Days without Money', stretching their last dollar to the very edge of absolute poverty:

> On one ten, never get caught again.
> I'll remember the days without money.
> This is senseless, awakening to poverty,
> as I journey into the days without money.

The contrast between the rich and the poor is illustrated again in 'One Student of Mine', which describes one "bright, cheerful, and dutiful" student of his "paying a quarter of a million dollars a year" to study in a college in the US while another child "at a street corner' in his neighbourhood "oversees a sweet-potato stove at night for her mother" because the mother "needs another couple of hundred dollars for the week". Lee's concern for the future of Hong Kong in the midst of this money ethos is conveyed starkly in 'Child of the Future':

> I hear your cry
> as your voice resonates from the chic
> metallic vest that you wear,
> through your palm-sized general-purpose
> computer
> to a prophet of the past
> about the extreme loneliness that you fear.

Though set in Hong Kong, the poem also describes the plight of children in other cities of the future, who, in spite of everything that can be possessed, do not know how to face the void in themselves.

A true poet, Lee does not leave readers with that emptiness but offers an alternative city, even if it may have been forgotten. In 'Forgotten Part of the City', he reminds us:

> Moss grows over an abandoned path.
> The lady bug repossesses its gloss
> from eye-blinding curtain walls.
> Life announces its return
> to a part of the city forgotten.

Even if the path is "abandoned", life can still return to it, as slowly but surely as the moss that grows. And in 'Ginger Flower Woman', he offers redemption in the fragrance of the ginger flower, well known in the city for its airy scent and its low cost, affordable even to people in humble circumstances:

> Slaughtered chickens hung by their nostrils,
> already skinned...
> raw fish lay with stretched-out bellies...
> I and these desolate beings, we exchanged glances,
> each contemplated the other's karma.
>
> In this tamed entanglement
> of life and death, of need and sacrifice,
> a woman passed by...
> she bought a stem of ginger flowers
> to decorate her humble steel and concrete home.

The return to a more livable life is offered not just to people in this city but also to other neighbours; in 'Masseuse in Shenzhen', Lee describes the masseuse's dignity in the art of her work:

> And in her very hands – a fine kinesthetic-
> tactile instrument –
> made for one single audience,
> on which she constantly redrew lines
> between intimacy, sensuality, and human
> dignity.

The alternative lifestyle that values life more than its trappings is succinctly captured in one of Lee's most quoted poems, 'The State of My House', in which "the spider weaves its web in stealth" and "ants tread trails' "surely and silently":

> When dust accumulates faster
> than a broom can sweep –
> then, it is a sign that ancient towering chaos
> has set in
> to claim its final victory.
>
> As paper piles up on my desk at an
> unprecedented rate,
> and as fashion changes faster than my mind
> can keep pace,
> life has finally opened her arms to the
> Pandorine embrace.

The spider, the ant, the dust, the papers and the person working at the desk can all co-exist in peace in the actualization of the inner life.

The collection as a whole takes us from one place to another, from Hong Kong to other places on the Pacific Coast and back again. In 'You Can Stay on this Ferry Forever', Lee promises, if you do not wish to disembark, you can ride it forever to scale "long stretches of sea without man," and "without land" "into life's undreamed-of places". For "only eleven Hong Kong dollars", this journey is for everyone, richer or poorer. While other people take the ferry to go somewhere, Elbert Lee has already arrived just by getting on.

Agnes S. L. Lam
July 2013

Sunshine and Rain on the Pacific Coast

In 'Before a Storm', the very first poem of this collection, the poet Elbert Siu Ping Lee writes:

> Musty air has laid siege to the city –
> it is here to stay...
>
> Against an expanding horizon of haze,
> red dragonflies descend
> to protest against the ineffective wind.
>
> I venture into the summer heat,
> to seek solace from a wandering crowd.

The poem alludes to historical as well as elemental forces that help shape the city of Hong Kong and its environment. As the brief description of the book on page two indicates, the poems in *Rain on the Pacific Coast* were written around the handover in 1997. Caught in the stillness before a storm, with the city besieged by forces outside its control, the speaker of the poem, like the *flâneur* in the poetry of Charles Baudelaire, seeks solace and inspiration from ordinary city life. The elemental forces of nature serve not as mere backdrop to the human drama depicted, but are enmeshed with the texture of poetry and with the life of the people.

The poet has a strong ecological sense. Cities nowadays are inevitably super shopping malls. The global economy has boosted consumerism that increasingly depletes the natural resources of the world. Specifically locating some of his poems in places like the IFC (International Finance Centre) in Central, or "Somecafe" in Causeway Bay, the poet challenges consumerism, and does so with a Buddhist bent in some poems. 'Statue of the Buddha' incorporates the clutter of goods in the poetry, and ends with an image of the Buddha on Lantau Island looking beyond the vending machines and litter, anticipating another eon that will bring in an alternative life and lifestyle.

Certain transformations of the Chinese and the English cultural heritage can be seen in the volume. In the deployment of images, the silkworm with its cocoon, a famous one in the poetry of the Tang Dynasty poet Li Shang Yin, metamorphoses to highlight a modern predicament:

> No peace for us.
> Restless.
> Every project, every worry
> binds us like silk around a cocoon.

There are also some short poems in this collection of poetry, poems that in style and form often echo the four-line regulated verse in Chinese poetry. The first instance of such short poems is the following:

> Tilted banana leaves
> on which rain-drops glide,
> writhe to the rhythm of the ancient two-string.
> My heart is lost to the wayward pleasures of
> the past.

By interspersing these single stanza poems amongst longer verses, the poet manages to create a rhythm even in the sequencing of poems. The brevity of these poems creates space for the reader's senses and imagination to roam and to relax, like taking a deep breath and exhaling gently after a brisk walk.

From the city's colonial past, a street named d'Aguilar boisterously enters the local scene, and gives a poem in the volume its distinctive rhythm, the insistence of which amounts to an accusation. Major General Sir George Charles D'Aguilar was Lieutenant Governor of Hong Kong in the mid-nineteenth century, but his name of Spanish origin, over a century later, has become ordinary fare and thoroughfare in Hong Kong. In the poem bearing the street name in its title, this fragment from colonial history provides the setting as well as the rhyming about the drudgery of life on a hard pavement in contemporary Hong Kong. A young hostess, working for a restaurant ironically named Heaven on Earth, has to stand for hours right outside it on d'Aguilar Street to get the attention of potential customers hurrying past. The poem ponders:

> Do you know what you are doing
> in d'Aguilar Street?
> Working all day
> in d'Aguilar Street.
>
> Getting lost
> in d'Aguilar Street.
> Losing your heaven on earth
> in d'Aguilar Street.
> What a way to make ends meet…
> in d'Aguilar Street.

In a city both burdened and enlightened by its past, life may be difficult, the air oppressive, and people awaiting a storm that brings an unpredictable outcome. But there can be an order in the ordinary, opening up paths to new vistas. Many poems in the volume appeal to a resilience in the natural world, in the human heart, in the common ways of people just walking around, observing, criticizing, sympathizing, so that we can seek solace in a wandering crowd, derive joy from poetry that sings of people, their relationships and their habitus, and trust in forces that will bring sometimes sunshine, sometimes rain to the Pacific Coast.

Ching Yuet May
October 2013

Rain on the Pacific Coast

Table of contents

Foreword by Agnes S. L. Lam	vii
Sunshine and Rain on the Pacific Coast by Ching Yuet May	xiii
Before a Storm	21
40M – Voyage of Distraction	22
Tilted banana leaves	23
Bamboo Grove	24
Blood Amber	25
Grave in the Catholic Cemetery	26
Live, as if …	27
Northern Light	28
Moments …	29
Ginger Flower Woman	30
Forgotten Part of the City	31
Our Daughters and Sons	32
Students and Teacher	33
When You Grow Up	34
How I …	35
Where Would I Be	36
Wet night…	37
The State of My House	38
Love in Life of Modernity	39
An Ode to a Departed Friend	40
Such stupid men …	42
Autumn Wind	43
Two Golden Monkeys	44
Masseuse in Shenzhen	45
Dongguan Karaoke	46
Let me love …	47
Bo Bo of Wuhan	48

One Student of Mine	50
City Chant	51
Each of us …	52
Between You and Me	53
New World	54
I am a species of God's maleness …	55
Statue of the Buddha	56
City of Life	58
Jenna Across the Skies	60
Highway 401	62
A Cold Evening	63
Rider of the Wind	64
New York Woman	66
Wall Lizard	67
Untitled I	68
Untitled II	69
Child of the Future	70
The Great Wah Fu Public Housing Estate	72
Siberian Moon	74
There is No Now Up Here	75
Corpus Animus	76
Blue Water Ash	77
Friends	78
Tai Tai Bodhisattva	80
D'Aguilar Street	82
Moving House	84
No peace for us …	85
Good Morning IFC	86
Facing the mighty city …	89
Days without Money	90
The quiet Moon …	93
You Can Stay on this Ferry Forever	94
Trees layered in fathoms …	95
My Husky is a Kitsune	96
One More Night	98

Sister Fairy Divine	100
When Will I See You Again	104
Missing Typhoon Megi	105
Tonight, a super full moon …	107
The Author	109
The Publishers	111
The International Proverse Prize for Unpublished Book-length Fiction, Non-fiction, or Poetry	112
The International Proverse Poetry Prize (single poems)	114
Poetry published by Proverse	116

Elbert Siu Ping Lee

☙ Before a Storm

Musty air has laid siege to the city –
it is here to stay...

Against an expanding horizon of haze,
red dragonflies descend
to protest against the ineffective wind.

I venture into the summer heat,
to seek solace from a wandering crowd.

            ❧   *IFC, Central*

✿ 40M – Voyage of Distraction

Her hair – sometimes she ties it back.
But whatever she does with it,
it is a new form of beauty,
a new prose,
a new song – written to overshadow
the golden rays of the setting sun.

Blue eyes – whether their shade
is the insignia of the evening sky,
or is a reflection of the ocean depth –
that I do not know.

Her gaze – it upsets my pretentious calm,
seeks a direct path to my heart,
and injects there the joy of life –
of that I am certain.

   Bonham Road, Mid Levels

Elbert Siu Ping Lee

☙
Tilted banana leaves
on which rain-drops glide,
writhe to the rhythm of the ancient two-
string.
My heart is lost to the wayward pleasures
of the past.

☙ Bamboo Grove

Ancestral urns sought shelter in a bamboo grove.
Banyan trees lent shade to rock-pile graves.
A path into the hidden hills was a path into time forgotten.

Falling leaves sailed against the angry wind.
White bones rattled, mountain spirits moaned...
for soon the iron caterpillar would begin to graze.

Uprooted is a community of time.
Buried is our past, our future,
the identity of the yellow face...
so the neon-lit mall can secure its clean and earthless way.

☙   *A Trail, Lamma Island*

Blood Amber

I sold my field
in order to buy twelve beads of blood-
amber.
Each a glowing cosmos of power and desire,
mouldering through time.

You and I are two tiny moths,
eternally consumed
by the recurring cosmoses of heat,
trapped in the twelve beads of blood-
amber.

    Pokfulam Village, Island West

Grave in the Catholic Cemetery

Angel on wings of marble,
with the pale face of Michelangelo's David,
bent to caress a soul....

On the grave-stone was a picture...
smooth dark hair, razor-sharp squinty eyes
not unlike those of a preying hawk,
set against a face well tried by time.

There lay the body of a person
born to a foreign territory in his homeland.
The angel's touch – was it a blessing or a curse?

Catholic Cemetery, Happy Valley

Elbert Siu Ping Lee

☙
Live, as if flesh is falling from your bones.
Make love, as if there is no tomorrow –
we have no more hope left to borrow from,
in our great leap into the future.

Northern Night

Thus rises the winter moon,
casting cold shadows on snow of blue.

In pale morning light,
contours of space undulate,
in tandem with our breathless gaze.

Silent movements awake,
to become brushes of heat
that paint life on a dim, water-colour
array.

In yet another deep dark space,
the car has been put to sleep...
together with the noise and worry
of the senseless day.

                           Markham, Toronto

Elbert Siu Ping Lee

☙

Moments of tenderness,
each standing alone,
subvert life-long projects.

Ginger Flower Woman

Slaughtered chickens hung by their nostrils,
already skinned...
raw fish lay with stretched-out bellies...
I and these desolate beings, we exchanged glances,
each contemplated the other's karma.

In this tamed entanglement
of life and death, of need and sacrifice,
a woman passed by...
she bought a stem of ginger flowers
to decorate her humble steel and concrete home.

        Wah Fu Market, Island South

❦ Forgotten Part of the City

Moss grows over an abandoned path.
The lady bug repossesses its gloss
from eye-blinding curtain walls.
Life announces its return
to a part of the city forgotten.

    ᭞   *Lady Clementi's Ride, Island South*

Our Daughters and Sons

Beauty has left the daughters of the city...

The little dragon,
ever since they began school,
has been creeping in,
stealing the blush from their cheeks
while they swotted away.

What the great economic miracle has also produced
is a generation of image-consuming drones,
a swarm of symbol-processing worker bees.
What can cosmetics and high fashion do
to a class of beings as deprived as these?

Admiralty, Central

Elbert Siu Ping Lee

Students and Teacher

My students are little beings
who have little regard for truth.

They never fail to hijack your attention,
when they do not ransack your affection.

When venomous,
they laugh at sages and spit at buddhas.
Their bellies are their gods.

Deceived and distractible,
they learn and they grow.

As for me, the teacher,
I can only learn how to be happily lost
in their presence.

Admiralty, Central

When You Grow Up

When you grow up,
I'll take you to that northern country,
where glittering highways traverse olive-
green fields in the summer sun.
You'd ask me why leaves are green.
I'd laugh, and you'd continue to ask.

Let us go, sister,
and ride through the motowns and
toetowns,
basking in their dry heat glory,
in the middle of nowhere,
like lost field lilies
racing to blossom and die
to escape winter's graven dawn.

Little princess, leave your sky palace –
an empty tower of concrete and power.
I'll show you beauty and love
in the ordinary...
then you will bathe boldly
in nameless street freedom.
You'd no longer ask.
Together we'd laugh.

Exchange Square, Central

ଓଃ
How I love the night,
no opinions, nor words.
My heart is at rest,
completely devoted to loving you.

❧ Where Would I Be

Where would I be without you, Muse? –
now that I have left the path of security,
of righteousness, and of good name.
I have abandoned all that I have learnt,
grasping no truth,
claiming no knowledge.

As a result,
I do not walk anymore in an upright
manner.
My body speaks the truth about the state of
my soul – it humps and bends,
as it occasionally sings and dances.

My mind constantly sings out sad songs,
not unlike the homing songs of humpback
whales – heard by no one,
except by those who tread a similar fate?

But at last, I am free – lost in the ocean of
faiths, horrific and heart-breaking, singing
my song –
am I further away, or am I closer to You?

     ❧ *Exchange Square, Central*

Elbert Siu Ping Lee

ଔ
Wet night…
My spirit rises with moist air,
only to find itself lost
in an empty embrace.

The State of My House

Evading your watchful gaze,
the spider weaves its web in stealth
in a neglected corner of your wall.

Below, surely and silently,
ants tread trails
as quickly as we can raise the insect spray.

When dust accumulates faster
than a broom can sweep –
then, it is a sign that ancient towering
chaos has set in
to claim its final victory.

As paper piles up on my desk at an
unprecedented rate,
and as fashion changes faster than my mind
can keep pace,
life has finally opened her arms to the
Pandorine embrace.

                    Wah Fu, Island South

Love in Life of Modernity

Where the sun sets,
there shall I be,
to seek love in the life of modernity –
where love has dissolved into a smile on a
piece of paper, plastered up on a wall
in a shopping mall,
frozen as if eternal.

Seek life from the face of a digital screen
where trees are greener, air is fresher
than what you can actually breathe.

I'd rather seek love in a lazy breeze in a
sunset that prepares way for the night,
where there are no smiles or faces to be
seen.

Seek life in an arid land,
abandoned for its poverty –
then we will find each other –
complete with sweat and tears.

Admiralty, Central

An Ode to a Departed Friend

Your spirit rushes through the shade of woods
where giant butterflies with folded wings
calmly feed on dead logs...

Now, you are finally freed
from cold, air-conditioned, neon-lit offices
in which humans and machines endlessly grind.

Twenty years have passed like the wind
since we met as neighbours.
Since then, we began to mingle
in socioeconomic relations we strained to understand,
shattered by forces called the Market.

Like broken clay in a trash bin
we were scattered,
unable to distinguish ourselves
from what was to be thrown away.

Now, your spirit regains its poise
as you find tranquility above places where
eagles circle.

Elbert Siu Ping Lee

This evening,
the lone fire in your front porch marks your departure.
It has remained despite the morning rain —
to remind us of something in life so unspeakable
that we choose not to remember,
but dare not forget.

      ಲ   *Pokfulam Trails, Island West*

ଔ
Such stupid men.
Tossed ashore by screaming waves,
they were scattered.
Some thought they could actually swim.

Autumn Wind

The autumn wind waves at me,
lifts up fallen leaves,
makes them dance as if to parade death.

Undeceived, I take stock of my possessions
and my possessions-to-be
and discover again
that our joys are indeed grown on the
ground of fear.

You summon a chill from my spine
as I try to regroup my shaken ambitions –
now broken into pieces beyond recognition.

But as I tenderly watch you blow,
I watch the epic movements of life come
to meet their enlightening end.

  Pokfulam Road, Island West

Two Golden Monkeys

I wish we were two golden monkeys.
Swinging from branches to branches we move,
in the deep of the forest,
away from traditions that are silent but
binding...

from marriage contracts and marriage
counseling...from fretting relatives...
away from evils that we cannot speak of.

I'd rather face the water pythons,
in the dark of the ravine,
with their protruding fangs,
so ostensibly frightening...
but then so tame and pathetic,
like you and me, ready to face extinction.

Swing away, partner!...
from the rule of company law,
from our intricate corporate planning,
and from the cannot-be-spoken-of horror
of securities and risk management.

Swing away...
from the snares of the primate soul,
into earth mother's dangerous haven.

                      Peel Rise, Island South

Elbert Siu Ping Lee

☙ Masseuse in Shenzhen

Her fingers landed on my forehead,
tenderly – about the meridian.
Feel...the touch of a strange Shenzhen
woman.

Tiny tapping fingers,
to which the contour of my face yielded its
secrets, gladly announced to the owner
about his previously deprived existence.

As she continued to play, to touch,
soma cells lined up –
about to march in columns.
Germ cells danced, nerve cells echoed,
firing in rhythm, to the direction of a great
40-yuan-an-hour concert master
whose name and life is tangential to that of
von Karajan.

And in her very hands – a fine kinesthetic-
tactile instrument –
made for one single audience,
on which she constantly redrew lines
between intimacy, sensuality, and human
dignity.

        ☙ *Somewhere, Shenzhen*

Dongguan Karaoke

Faces of Nymphs and Artemises break into
crowded Karaoke space.
The night ritual begins
as luring eye shadows compete and insinuate.

Hearts panting and palms sweating –
these are the only unmistakable symptoms of
that not-so-real time and place –
but what justifies the need to judge
what is real and what is fake?

For soon, our calculative gazes will be thrown
into disarray
as music and voice go their own ways!

Are we here to seek love?
Or, is this a programmed ritual to mate?

         ∂ *Somekaraoke, Dongguan*

Elbert Siu Ping Lee

ଓ
Let me love you briefly,
like dew visiting a morning leaf;
gone, as you blossom with the rising sun.

Bo Bo of Wuhan

How I took you to my room
when the party was over
as cracked voices and bland music
dissipated in sombre space.

How we broke the second silence
and overcame the estrangedness
of heritage, language, and years,
of a dubious transaction,
of impending biological havoc.

Then you lay before me
fully extending your large frame
when your milk-white skin
blended in with the fragrance of a newly
laundered sheet.

Reluctantly, we sent our words,
like sentinels forever probing forward,
cautiously preparing for the advent of
a not-to-be-easily-lost brigade of tongues
and other kinds of flesh.

For some moments,
we met as humans fully alive
bridging the haunting distance between
two wandering souls
lost in their twisted career paths that
would only lose to heal.

At the command of break of day we had to
part, we knew,
like the Cowherd and the Weaver who meet
once
for a day in a thousand years on a path less
travelled,
in the deep fathoms of space.

     ࿇   *Somehotel, Wuhan*

One Student of Mine

From a school of a diocese,
one student of mine is going to a well-to-do
college in the U.S.
paying a quarter of a million dollars a year.
She is bright, cheerful, and dutiful.
I rated her potential high.

At a street corner around my
neighbourhood, a child of God
oversees a sweet-potato stove at night for
her mother
who needs another couple of hundred
dollars for the week.
Does she know what extra-curricular
activities should be like!
Whose potential have we denied?

One tear-drop fell from my eyes.
The other, evaporated by an
incomprehensible reality
has engulfed this ignorant city.

                    Wah Fu, Island South

City Chant

Computations go on and on…
day and night
like aimless souls wandering
so aimlessly
according to schedule
on highways and telephone lines and

the clockwork has been strengthened
by the dictation of a more-and-more perfect
formula, so comparably impeccably neat
and relatively justifiable that
only flip-flop souls can inhabit

to produce ever-better results
to almost satisfy the appetite
of the changing needs
of a grander building
or the evolving demands
of a project of seeming excellence
requiring thousands more aimless souls
with flip-flop minds
and millions and trillions of computations
to go on and on, day and night
like aimless souls wandering…

            ❧   *IFC, Central*

ଓଃ
Each of us tried to grasp a full handful.
We quickly shoved it into our mouths.
There was nothing except sand and dirt.
We looked around and started to boast –
humbly, about our achievements.

Elbert Siu Ping Lee

❦ Between You and Me

Between You and Me, there lies
an expanse of troubled waters
that stretches from North to South.

Between us is a river of time with precipices and rapids,
shaping our histories, our nights and days.
Where do we stand –
along those long and rough river banks?

Between us is a deep abyss of uncertainty,
too deep and too wide even for a giant's stride.

Between us is the flaming sword
that guards the garden of Eden,
held by Cherubim and sharp-eyed angels holy and divine.

The only thing that holds us together
are the gentle hands of the carpenter's son –
those coarse and stigmatized hands that hold
a fractured world together.

❧   *Markham, Toronto*

New World

Lifeless hum of turning tires,
colourless nauseating fumes,
steel cocoons on the move;
some rattle, some soar.

Machine termites migrating
from sunrise to sunset
on germ-free rubber-coated highways.

Mind-laming motion,
mind-numbing speed,
clockwork motions of death...
directed, concerted,
by lifeless beings in need.

Don Valley Parkway, Toronto

Elbert Siu Ping Lee

Ͽℨ
I am a species of God's maleness,
visiting your pale and luscious body –
the mirror image of Tara,
with her unveiled mountains and valleys,
poised to receive summer rain from
heaven.

Statue of the Buddha

Seemingly unmoved by the clouds behind him,
unmoved by the crowd rushing
in and out of his sight,
sat the great statue of the Buddha of Lantau.

He did not seem annoyed
by the array of vending machines
and the perpetual feast that took place
underneath his lotus seat,
the occasional flash of an automatic Nikon
or its like.

He was not disturbed by the littering
children, who played under his feet,
or by absent-minded adults
in their failed pilgrimage, unwary of this fact.

His long ears drooped to listen
to the myriad of chants, broadcast
out of sync via a thousand tiny electronic prayer machines,
sold on the road-side
to those too busy or too distracted to pray.

The world swirled above him and below.
Yet he did not lose his composure,
unswayed by the lost crowd.
There he sat, facing east,
for another eon to come.

> *Phoenix 'Sunset Peak' Trail,*
> *Lantau Island*

City of Life

Young faces move in a hurry,
to check out another consumer item,
failing completely
to meet each other.
Gasping gently
through lungs embalmed
in a spicy mix of petrol fume
and ever-present dust,
wide-open mouths flow out words of
ignorance.

Old bodies falter not,
if wealthy.
They emit an eerie glow,
and continue to go to their offices –
by grace of some heaven-endowed organic
root,
like ailing gods who refuse to die –
to hoard more real estate.

Dolphins flee
from rivers and deltas,
avoiding bleeding wastes,
bringing with them saner fish,
to seek shelter in undisturbed bays.

Elbert Siu Ping Lee

Shiny green beetles continuously disappear
along with red and blue dragonflies,
as they seek sanctuary
through sealed, tempered-glass windows,
finding death instead.

Heat waves surge
to devour without mercy
pale bodies and fragile minds preserved in
air-conditioned galleries.

Ladies and gentlemen,
may I present to you the Pearl of the
Orient,
The City of Life!

        ঌ   *Exchange Square, Central*

Jenna Across the Skies

Here
there are many miles of highways.
But none of them can bring me to you.

In the night, solitary signs flicker.
I trespass crossings, I stop at lights,
I drive like a mad fool.
But where are you?

In that deep darkness –
the disappearance of hope –
I face humanity's final truth.
A fragment of it is finding you.

When will I go home?
A slave in a foreign country,
a slave to myself, a slave to many.

Freedom and liberation,
when will you bring me to my love –
my companion of all times,
my child and my friend?

Elbert Siu Ping Lee

Yes,
I miss our moments together;
a movie or a cup of tea.
They are very, very precious to me.
Your eyes and your smile,
in skies and clouds I see.

       ے *14th Avenue, Markham*

Highway 401

A fragment of rainbow
left behind by a carefree angel,
descends to bestow blessings on those
who look up to the autumn sky.

Seagulls gather, some standing on one leg,
against that cold westerly,
to pick up crumbs fallen from the hands
of distracted minds heading east,
toward that foreign-language city.

Here at this juncture, we meet and part,
traveling in parallel,
each in our own ways.
None of us shall meet again, perhaps never,
not until that very final day.

I hear them shriek, the seagulls.
They seem to be saying,
"No more crumbs from heaven
to feed those who are too busy making a living."

Highway 401, Ontario

A Cold Evening

The north wind screamed,
rushed across the hinterland of snow,
of leafless trees.
Shimmering lights decorated the darkening city.
Vehicles travelled hastily –
as if desperate to seek something –
all hurrying home.

I watched every movement, every colour, shape,
in silence.
I watched the world standing on its own –
a world struggling.
Alas, glorious but lonely city,
where was it heading to –
in the boundless, matterless, dark universe.

Scorched by a severe yet crushed beauty,
my eyes turned to those who were near.
My heart yearned for a touch of deep humanity,
to fill this breathlessly unbridled void.

        St. Laurent, Montreal

Rider of the Wind

I am the rider of the wind.
I come from nowhere and I go nowhere,
never become tired.

My eyes have seen plenty.
I have seen comets
etching curved metallic lines across
the dim evening sky.

But I know that those who make a wish on
such a sight,
will see their wish vanish
as quickly as the bright trail the comet
leaves behind.

I have seen the moon in all her graceful
postures –
crescent, half, and full.
Slowly, but certainly, it traverses the deep
dark horizon.

I am a friend of the moon
that causes people to become sad,
and sometimes to act wild.
But I know the moon only pulls the tide.

Elbert Siu Ping Lee

Have you ever seen the nebula,
dense as she is sparse?
Those eyes that are caught in her
are lost in a dizziness not different from
that of our own lives –
so apparent, yet so incomprehensible.
She draws us to her like a veiled guide.

Let us not forget the evening sun
that sets early on a winter day.
That red and mesmerizing glow –
a joy to the eyes of mortals –
yet a sign of their quickened fate?

I, the rider of the wind, am here to stay,
to watch the comets,
to stare at the moon in her beguiling
postures,
to survey the nebula, and to feel the
warmth of the setting sun with you.

    ☙   *Sassoon Road, Island South*

New York Woman

She came from New York.
There she sits,
in the corner of a bar
almost every day.

Between her index and middle fingers,
a cigarette is burning away
like her life here
burning away
alone,
like you and me
burning away
alone.

The occasional smile on her face
does not stop her from appearing
to be waiting for someone or something —
a boy, a man, a woman, a girl, a child, a
cat, or a dog,
to give her
the longest, deepest, and gravest hug
of her life.

Somebar, Causeway Bay

Elbert Siu Ping Lee

෴
Wall Lizard

Visiting your room silently at night,
I watch
your sweet countenance,
refusing to be dimmed
by fading lantern light.

Free from the torment of human passion,
I watch you completely
purely, sincerely.

I long to slither across the ceiling,
slide along the beam,
yearn to listen to your light breathing.

Freely and unreservedly,
you reveal yourself to me –
a cold-blooded creature, half-hiding –
whose heart gently pounds
at the instance of my sight.

    ૐ *Wah Fu, Island South*

☙ Untitled I
Poem by Tang Dynasty poet Li Shang Yin. Translation.

Beyond the layers of veils
that surround your back court love
chamber,
alone you wait in the lingering dawn.

A deva caught in her own woven dream,
forgetting that you, sister,
dwell in a man-forbidden realm.

A caltrop reed will not hold back foaming
waves;
dew drops will not fail to accentuate the
sweet scent of osmanthus.

Do I not feel the leading-to-nowhere blues?
But the sorrow of loving you, sister,
is enlightening madness.

           ❧   *Wah Fu, Island South*

Untitled II
Poem by Tang Dynasty poet Li Shang Yin. Translation.

How can I choose between the two pains:
that of not seeing you and
that of leaving you?
How can flowers blossom,
when the east wind fails to bring rain?

A silkworm will not die
before it exhausts itself in its cocoon;
Nor will my tears dry
before the night candle turns to ash.

Anxiously, I watch myself go through time
in the morning mirror.
Weeping in the dark can be cold indeed
under frost-bitten moonlight.

There are not many paths
that lead to your mountain, I know.
My hope, let it rest on the peeking green bird
that shuttles between our homes at night.

        Wah Fu, Island South

Child of the Future

I hear your cry
as your voice resonates from the chic
metallic vest that you wear,
through your palm-sized general-purpose
computer
to a prophet of the past
about the extreme loneliness that you fear.

You rummage through your intricate family
of belongings,
and you wade through the countless
services you can acquire –
more than any child in the past could
dream of.
In them you find marginal pleasure but
absolutely no joy.
All day long, you march in your little
kingdom of boredom
which you share with no-one.

I see in your visage – that for the man in a
child who will not become the child in a
man – there will not be any growing up.
For you already know so well what you
want,
so well-equipped for the future
that your parents and teachers are dying to
prepare you for.

Elbert Siu Ping Lee

You stumble through life, despite your
exquisite knowledge,
like a blind man without hands
you trip and fall as you win battles
against the others,
like a mad knight,
fighting homeless spirits as they call.
But in all these triumphs you fail to find
your own worth.

I can feel the fatigue
that has haunted you since you were small;
your loneliness, your absent-mindedness,
and your desperation, so massive that one
is tempted to think
you are without parents.
Like you, I am not sure what parenting
means any more.

You will grow up only
by finding that child in you
that creative, merciful, and compassionate
child in you, and in one another.
Only then, the heavens will open up and
the earth will heal
and you will no longer be bored.

    ❧ *Admiralty, Central*

The Great Wah Fu Public Housing Estate

There it is,
an unmistakable extension of
the autumn sky,
a back chamber to nurse those
who have lost their pride.

Hiding in recesses of the southern heights,
your not-so-fair complexion fails
to catch the eyes of passers-by.

Winding corridors,
made treacherously longer by ever-dimming
lights,
harbour the playground for children in
plight.

Lone stairways,
stretching ever steeper,
form a challenge
for early-retiring adults without insight.

Where are you taking us
you great monument of urban decadence?

Keeping us warm,
keeping us in,
keeping us from the nuisance
of metropolitan life.

Saving and damning us, Wah Fu,
together we paint a picture of raw urban
delight.

         ❧   *Wah Fu, Island South*

❃ Siberian Moon

Siberian Moon,
I saw one.
Across the ocean of clouds,
winced.

Visitors on titanium wings beware:
between destinations,
between the earth and the stars,
an expanse of alien beauty resists,
unconquered
in a land of turbid air, vapour, and fumes.

   Urumqi air space

There is No Now Up Here

There is no now
up here
10 kilometers above the ground,
coaxed by head winds and tail winds
into lingering memories of the past
and anxieties of things that not yet are.

There is no room
for my body,
no quiet flushing water for leisure and pleasure
ten kilometers above the ground,
wrapped in a tube tight and linear
skipping across cosmic space unbound.

A generation traveling mean and fast…
Are we getting anywhere?

> *Urumqi air space*

ಛ Corpus Animus

Your lovely body has
moved sales,
kept gazes,
inspired the shape of bottles and cars,
sometimes even
redefined the meaning of magazines and
papers.

But for some reason,
you have forgotten to nourish
the fields and valleys,
the quiet streams and ravines.

Therefore,
the mulberry bush withers,
lands parch,
ice caps melt,
air turns into fume and forests vanish.

Because of your forgetfulness, goddess,
the stream of being comes to
an abrupt end.

           ઓ   *Somebar, Causeway Bay*

Blue Water Ash

You gently swirled
as I emptied you into the blue water of
Wong Chuk Kok Sea.

Your ash spiraled away
like a galaxy finding its home
in the translucent void.

Dear grandmother,
no grave, no urn,
nothing should contain your spirit and life,
only the unfathomable deep.

Blue water, white bone, white ash –
teach me my endearing teachers:
The moment is eternal,
but passes in a flash.

You came as a light to the world,
now you are extinguished.
Blessed is the Sutras' wish.

      Wong Chuk Kok Sea, Plover Cove

Friends

Holding hands
we walk into impermanence
as friends.

We – fragments of each other –
left in each other's memory
weave our selves into existence.

We – faces appearing strange yet familiar –
once said childhood lullabies together
at a time we no longer ponder.

In many directions we go
always changing paths.
Now young, now old,
now grasping, now ready to let go,

All sailing in the sea of conditioned arising
where metal, wood, water, fire, earth mix
and personalities unfold

Like horrid drag tides
drawing all
towards a distant shore
whose story we do not know.

From me to you,
from being to being,
from transience to transience,
runs a thread of compassion along which
all alien forms meander.

  అ *Somecafe, Causeway Bay*

Tai Tai Bodhisattva

Wandering in the mall
you move gracefully
in your occasion-perfect outfit.
At your sight, I hold my breath
treading my path of faith
in the crowd's midst.

This is the routine you go through
from day to day –
casting beautiful reflections
on shop floors and glass displays.
This is your work, this is your faith.

I keep my silence as I meditate
from place to place
casting doubt on the proceeds
of your day.
This is my work, this is my way.

Through your lips
blossom speeches of angelic accent
spoken with the precision
of a teutonic gauge – you pause, at times,
to remind us that we are
only laymen in our mundane presence.

In my mind,
a language of karmic accident
reflecting nothing but cosmic dissonance.
I waver, at times,
being aware that we still share
the same table, same bread, same
nuisance.

Near the day's end,
in a matter-of-fact manner,
you draw out your fan of cards
to mark the end of your royal charade.
And I – I try to keep my manners,
to live without too much disgrace
in this God-forsaken place.

    ≈   *Queen's Road Central, Central*

D'Aguilar Street

Standing outside Heaven on Earth
in d'Aguilar Street.
It's only a Chinese restaurant
in d'Aguilar Street.

You are only seventeen
in d'Aguilar Street.
Do you not feel the summer heat
in d'Aguilar Street?

Standing there from five till eleven
in d'Aguilar Street.
Wearing a smile like that of the fairy queen
in d'Aguilar Street.

Trying to catch peoples' eyes
in d'Aguilar Street.
Trying to avoid stares
in d'Aguilar Street.

From across the street, I can feel your
heart beat!

Elbert Siu Ping Lee

Do you know what you are doing
in d'Aguilar Street?
Working all day
in d'Aguilar Street.

Getting lost
in d'Aguilar Street.
Losing your heaven on earth
in d'Aguilar Street.

What a way to make ends meet…
in d'Aguilar Street.

        ✒   *d'Aguilar Street, Central*

Moving House

Lifting dust-covered tables...
I don't want to move but I have to go.
Packing and unpacking albums of photos...
Is this really the person I know?

Ruminating unfinished fables...
Don't you think, this is just a big show?
You and I and more to tangle and
untangle...
I know, I don't know, but I have to go.

Here lies a box, where lie secrets yet to be told.
I pour a cup of coffee to calm the domestic rubble...
Clearing my house, ruffling my soul till it's upside-down.
Sitting on a stool, taking a rest from categorized chaos...

Little doggie, watching me upheave time...
Lying down, cowering –
can your little nose smell
who will be the talk of the town?

Wah Fu, Island South

Elbert Siu Ping Lee

❦
No peace for us.
Restless.
Every project, every worry,
birds us like silk around a cocoon.

Good Morning IFC

Bonjour, L'Occitane
pour qui avez vous fait
la demain?
Are you a foe or a friend?

I am not Estee Lauderian.
But your models' lush eye lashes will
make me one, for certain.

Hello there, Gucci bag.
You have turned departed cows into a
luxury item.
I'd like to carry one away.
Will I make it without writing a cheque?

Got to go to Body Shop
before I start to look a flop.
"You can return the plastic bottles here!
and look like a snob!"

What about you Calvin Klein?
Tight cotton undies wrapped on nubile
bodies.
How can I decline?
You are nothing short of divine.

Elbert Siu Ping Lee

Vous êtes Alain Figaret?
Mon plaisir a vous rencontrer.
A jacket, a shirt, a tie.
They will help me make my day.

There you are, Cerrutti.
Are you from France or from Italy?
I'll come back to you when I have more money.
But sorry, today you are just unlucky.

Dear Kwanpen,
lizard keeper and crocodile fiend.
Skin them beautifully, skin them live.
Make suitcases for our women and our men.

Fcuk or Fkuc or whatever it may be –
a name so hard to say.
What if your u is placed before your c?
Then I'll say your name more easily.

Konichiwa, Asura Tayama.
This is certainly Japanese, I can tell my mama. What do you sell exactly?
This is beyond my karma.

Gently, gently, Burberry.
A raincoat so chic that it is a luxury.
Because you are not really made for the needy,
you've become our ladies' ecstasy.

Rain on the Pacific Coast

Hello, Tiffany & Co –
distant and cold.
You only sell silver and gold.
Wow, wearing you is simply a great show.

Salut, chere Clinique.
Peau blanc, mon petit.
Peau blanc, mon petit.
I'm telling you, that's all you need.

Here you go, Godiva.
Chocolate, sugar, and plague tartar –
our privileged children's favourite dose
as they tread on life's grand boulevard.

Oh no, Macdonald's!
big macs and salted potatoes.
Do you have some more for those
who are always on the road?

Good morning, IFC
I have seen what I needed to see.
Our civilzation's masterpiece.
But it subsides in smog and turbid breeze
as I ferry back to lower realms
to kiss my two dogs' tender ears.

                ❧   *IFC, Central*

ଔ
Facing the mighty city, I bow.
I fear. – Will I succeed, or will I drift into oblivion?

Days without Money

I'll remember the days without money
when Wednesdays were empty and
Saturdays were Saturn heavy.

In the bank,
You are down to two hundred and sixty.
On the days without money,
how are you going to feed your family?

Do not fall into the days without money.
Your friends will leave you and
so will your little honey.

In your pocket, five sixty.
You will have to decide whether to read
today's news
or save some money for the crying baby
on the days without money.

Debtors call, self-appointed helpers knock
on the door on your days without money.
Bank loans glow in the dark,
control freaks take over,
help becomes schemes of risk management,
on your days without money.

Elbert Siu Ping Lee

Stare hard, when you are left with two sixty.
Buy packet noodles not iPods
if you want to survive
the days without money.

Skies twirl, clouds fumble
Stomachs turn, ulcers burn –
angry, you cannot think clearly
on the days without money.

Sit tight on the days without money.
If you are only managing a day with two twenty,
Sit tight, before you start to wonder if you are the guilty party,
before everybody thinks it is your karmic destiny.

Two more weeks to go, on the days without money.
Time stops, there is no sign any cheque will arrive.
Jobs hide, calls will take you for a ride
on the days without money.
Remember, never lose your sanity.

When you stay afloat with one eighty,
things start to go kinky.
Bills are ever punctual and they grow manifold.
Credit cards fry, bank notes dive,
if you cannot run away from the days
without money.

Get drunk on cheap beer –
a six-pack for only twelve fifty –
a certain and affordable getaway
from the days without money.
But don't forget you only have one eighty.

On one sixty, you step into ghost realms.
Hell laughs, dogs howl, cats burrow,
lizards starve on naked walls,
on your hardest days without money.

On one ten, never get caught again.
I'll remember the days without money.
This is senseless, awakening to poverty,
as I journey into the days without money.

         ≈   *Tai Wo, Peng Chau Island*

Elbert Siu Ping Lee

ଓ
The quiet Moon,
like a tainted silver disk,
glides across an empty dark sky –
leaving no trace.

☙ You Can Stay on this Ferry Forever

You can stay on this ferry forever,
surfing waves, shuttling between Lantau,
Cheung Chau, Peng Chau
and other tiny islands near and far.

I can stay on this ferry forever – each night –
star gazing, slacking, forever orbiting
around a shining metropolis – oh so near
but so far – never reaching its busy piers.

You can stay on this ferry forever,
scaling long stretches of sea without man,
without land,
watching the city
now glowing, now fading, now sinking –
in sync with the daily headlines.

We can stay on this ferry forever –
on this steel and plastic honey called Ming

River, for only eleven Hong Kong dollars,
never getting tired
of riding this slow ferry – precious vehicle for hire as we venture
into life's undreamed-of places.

 ❧   *Inter-island ferry*

Elbert Siu Ping Lee

ଔ
Trees layered in fathoms
arch the cold distance,
cast shadows that dance to the music of
the lazy wind.

My Husky is a Kitsune

My husky is a kitsune.
Not old –
between a thousand years and three.

My husky is a kitsune –
the right hand of Tara,
sent to keep me company on my life-
journey.

My husky is a kitsune.
Armed with steel claws, a pointy nose, and
radar ears –
she has disguised herself as a Siberian
Husky!

When she was twenty months old and still a
baby,
I brought her home from the local vet's.
She appeared to me in a dream –
a celestial general with the full moon as
her canopy.

Wherever I go,
she keeps me company.
To everyone I know,
She is both untamed and friendly.
She indulges in vanilla ice cream and other
forbidden goodies.

Not always polite, she pisses on IFC
walkways.
Wild and fierce, she disregards human
taboos, superficial dignity.
Whatever she does, she is my beloved
husky kitsune.

She will bring me
fame, fortune, and great wisdom.
She will find me my dearest honey.
It's been a long hard journey,
dear kitsune.

Kitsune, you have already been following
me for a thousand years.
Will we meet again
in some far-away place
in another thousand years?

        ಞ   *Wah Fu, Island South*

One More Night

One more night,
one more solitary night
together, as we bathe
in mist-stricken IFC light – forever glowing.

There is so little time in this life
to spend alone with you,
in a dark world,
in gentle breathing,
with hearts tip-toeing;
not drunk,
not on Panadol,
not thinking.

We love as pure male and female beings –
without jobs or positions,
like our canine companions
now abiding in a hidden quarter of our
dwelling;
sleeping,
dreaming,
ruminating.

Elbert Siu Ping Lee

In this shabby stone house
on a forgotten island,
at a time when machines slumber,
we break the word barrier,
with eyes open,
to ravish silent songs in the dark
for one more solitary night.

           ❧   *Peng Chau, Islands*

Sister Fairy Divine

On this tiny island you reside
with your simple family.
You try to envelop your developing body
in worn out T-shirts and large nighties –
and you walk high.

You are kind
and your are a child.
I am your teacher
but you are my prime tutor of unbound
samsaric measure.
Riding beside you are the twin waves
of unchecked passion and free flowing
grace.
Human mortals stay away!

Your left hand holds
the sceptre of possible triangulations
and your right hand
the threat of incessant multiple relations.
Jealousy you drink as wine
with the innocence of the Madonna's child.
Are you human?
Or is the Fairy your Sister and the Temple
your home?

Elbert Siu Ping Lee

Have you come, Sister Fairy,
to reveal beauty and mercy?
Or, is your heavenly task to subdue men's
desire gone wild?
You are a true soulmate.
But then, with your smile,
all men confess their hearts to you.
Is this a blessing or is it a crime?

Only nineteen, clasped in simple clothing,
cosmetics and make up. – Men beg your
notice.
Unusual for your age, you own no iPods, no
touch-screen mobiles.
Where do you come from?
Only Secondary Five,
yet you speak like a fairy queen in disguise.

On seeing your face,
generals abandon their armour and flee.
Squadrons crumble; there will be no battle.
Surrounding you are heroes,
now all self-imposed slaves.
Whether they stay or run,
All lose the game.
Among us, the new Yang Guifei.

Is this your equation of love –
the greatest joy is delivered with the
greatest pain?
I would not call this love a zero sum game,
especially if you hold the buttons to deliver
pain.

Archetypal femininity in sharp display –
you throw every man's hope into disarray.
A hydro nuclear blast in assembly –
one day, we will all feel radioactive decay
–
human mortals and tiny communities.
Whatever you do, dear Sister,
never leave us to yearn alone in an eternal
void –
do not keep us at bay.

But tonight, I'll put on my paper armour.
I'll mount my feather lance.
Like a mad knight,
I'll declare independence
from your majesty's state sovereign,
become a broken raft in the boundless sea
of desire.
Thank you for your lessons, but I am also
your teacher
of equal samsaric measure –
what you need to know is still precious in
my mind.

Elbert Siu Ping Lee

The next time we meet,
it will be on a ferry on a distant star, not at
a social work agency;
beyond the galaxies.
We have already traversed a million phases
of the time-weary moon –
to get here,
dear Sister Fairy Divine.

        ☙   *Peng Chau, Islands*

Rain on the Pacific Coast

☙ When Will I See You Again

When will I see you again
on this crowded ferry?

When I start to talk,
you throw me an orange, or a banana, or
a magazine that I cannot read;
all to shut me up.

When will we meet the next time
on this rush-hour ferry?

With you sitting next to me,
sister divine,
the 6 o'clock ferry becomes gossip time.
But I can hear nothing
when your eyes stare into mine.

When will we speak to each other again as friends
on this desolate ferry?

When a tiresome crowd
ends another directionless daily shuttle,
your ivory white hands, clasping mine,
will signal my life of searching has finally
come to an end.

☙ *Peng Chau, Islands*

Elbert Siu Ping Lee

☙ Missing Typhoon Megi

So, you may not come this way —
our way,
to this city,
this sleepless city of eyes wide open at night,
greeting cameras and all kinds of displays —
made for our eyes only.

In our realm,
we stare into eyes that cannot see.
We pose for cameras that cannot breathe.
That's what we do.

Our immortal artificial vision from high
tracks that one eye, carefully —
your eye,
the moving eye of the storm,
as you orchestrate a wild dance of black
clouds kilometers across.

Twenty four hours a day,
we keep on taking pictures
of things big and small.
In a week, you will complete the journey of
your graceful life, carelessly —
knocking down people and trees.

Rain on the Pacific Coast

You do not blink.
Nor do you linger,
or wait, or stay, or delay.

This time we will not see your splendour –
that empty eye of the storm
at the centre of which time stands still, they say.

As we try to capture more with our cameras
and our many other video devices,
your singular eye will continue to scan the
unfathomable deep blue of the Pacific,
from ten thousand meters high
leaving our grand and tiny visions behind.

Megi, there will be a time
when all the other eyes are closed,
then, maybe, our eyes will become like
yours –
capable of scanning the unfathomable
deep blue of people, of life.

As we look into each other's eyes this time –
I know we will not see each other again in this life, Megi.
So, goodbye.

      ❧   *Peng Chau, Islands*

Elbert Siu Ping Lee

ങ
Tonight, a super full moon
rules the horizon
as fluid shadows dance on the singular path
that leads to the other side,
at a dark moment
of earth time.

ങ ങ ങ

THE AUTHOR

Elbert Lee was raised in Hong Kong at a time when water shortages and shared flats were common. It was also a time when toys were made from popsicle-sticks and cigarette boxes. Spending a great deal of time in the New Territory countryside (he attended Fung Kai Primary school in Sheung Shui), he grew up with mud-covered pigs that obstructed village walkways.

In his secondary school years, he studied at St. Joseph's College, a school run by the La Salle brothers of Ireland. There, he had his first encounter with religious teachings and literature in English. Both subjects fascinated him. In literature, he was especially impressed by the works of Yeats who to him was the tragic poet hero par excellence.

Shortly after his graduation he went to study at McGill University in Montreal, Canada. Upon returning to Hong Kong, he worked briefly in the business sector after which he continued studies at the master's level at the University of Hong Kong. Upon graduation, he taught briefly at the then City Polytechnic before he took up further studies in New Zealand.

At the University of Auckland, he became a lay member of the Franciscan community where he was first introduced to Christian mysticism. He ran a newsletter in the community and was exposed to the works of Thomas Merton and those of other Catholic monastic writers. It was then that he became interested in poetry again: some of his earliest poems were published in the newsletter.

Elbert left New Zealand to join his family in Toronto in Canada a few years before Hong Kong's change-over. There, he worked briefly as a research associate at the University of Toronto and at other business organizations.

He returned to Hong Kong to witness the change-over and served in the private education sector for a few years. It was during these turbulent years that he found time to contemplate and to read about Taoism and Buddhism. It was also during these years that he started to write poems in a more systematic and disciplined way.

His poems have appeared in a number of magazines and e-journals.

THE PUBLISHERS

Proverse Hong Kong (PVHK), founded by Gillian and Verner Bickley, is based in Hong Kong with long-term and developing regional and international connections.

We have published novels, novellas, non-fiction (including autobiography and biography, history, memoirs, sport, travel narratives), single-author poetry collections, children's, young teens and academic books. Other interests include diaries, and academic works in the humanities, social sciences, cultural studies, linguistics and education. Some Proverse books have accompanying audio texts. Some are translated into Chinese.

We welcome authors who have a story to tell, wisdom, perceptions or information to convey, a person they want to memorialize, a neglect they want to remedy, a record they want to correct, a strong interest that they want to share, skills they want to teach, and who consciously seek to make a contribution to society in an informative, interesting and well-written way. Proverse works with texts by non-native-speaker writers of English as well as by native English-speaking writers.

The name "Proverse", combines the words "prose" and "verse" and is pronounced accordingly.

THE INTERNATIONAL PROVERSE PRIZE FOR UNPUBLISHED BOOK-LENGTH FICTION, NON-FICTION OR POETRY

The Proverse Prize, an annual international competition for an unpublished single-author book-length work of fiction, non-fiction, or poetry, the original work of the entrant, submitted in English (translations welcomed) was established in January 2008. It is open to all who are at least eighteen on the date they sign the entry form and without restriction of nationality, residence or citizenship.

Founded by Gillian and Verner Bickley, the objectives of the prize are: to encourage excellence and / or excellence and usefulness in publishable written work in the English Language, which can, in varying degrees, "delight and instruct". Entries are invited from anywhere in the world.

The Prize
1) Publication by Proverse Hong Kong, with
2) Cash prize of HKD10,000 (HKD7.80 = approx. USD1.00)

Extent of the Manuscript: within the range of what is usual for the genre of the work submitted. However, it is advisable that novellas be in the range, 30,000 to 45,000 words; other fiction (e.g. novels, short-story collections) and non-fiction (e.g. autobiographies, biographies, diaries, letters, memoirs, essay collections, etc.) should be in the range, 75,000 to 100,000 words. Poetry collections should be in the range, 5,000 to 25,000 words. Other word-counts and mixed-genre submissions are not ruled out.

Annual Entry Deadlines (subject to confirmation and/or change)

Receipt of Entry Fees / Entry Forms begins	[Variable, no later than] 14 April
Deadline for receipt of Entry Fees / Entry Forms	31 May
Receipt of entered manuscripts begins	1 May
Deadline for receipt of entered manuscripts	30 June

More information, updated from time to time, is available on the Proverse website: proversepublishing.com

THE INTERNATIONAL PROVERSE POETRY PRIZE
(SINGLE POEMS)

An annual international Proverse Poetry Prize (for single poems) was established in 2016.

The international Proverse Poetry Prize is open to all who are at least eighteen years old whatever their residence, nationality or citizenship.

Single poems, submitted in English, are invited on (a) <u>any subject or theme, chosen by the writer</u> OR (b) <u>on a subject or theme selected by the organisers.</u>

Poems may be in any form, style or genre. Each poem should be no more than 30 lines.

Entries should previously be unpublished in any way (except in the case of unpublished translations into English of the entrant's own work already published in another language, providing the entrant holds the copyright).

Entrants keep their copyright.

In 2016, cash prizes were offered as follows:
1st prize; USD100.00; 2nd prize: USD45.00; 3rd prizes (up to four winners): USD20.00.

If there are enough good entries in any year, an anthology of prize-winners and selected other entries will be published.

In 2016, judging took place at the same time as the judging for the Proverse Prize for unpublished book-length fiction, non-fiction or poetry.

Judges: anonymous (as for the Proverse Prize for an unpublished book-length work).

Max number of entries per person: No maximum. No poet may win more than one prize.

The above information is for guidance only.

More information, updated from time to time, is available on the Proverse website:
proversepublishing.com

POETRY PUBLISHED BY PROVERSE

Those who enjoy **Rain on the Pacific Coast** may also enjoy the following.

Alphabet, by Andrew S Guthrie, 2014.

Astra and Sebastian, by L.W. Illsley.

Chasing Light, by Patricia Glinton-Meicholas. , November 2013.

China suite and other poems, by Gillian Bickley. November 2009.

For the record and other poems of Hong Kong, by Gillian Bickley. 2003.

Freda Kahlo's Cry and Other Poems, by Laura Solomon, 2015.

Heart to Heart, by Patty Ho, 2010.

Home, away, elsewhere, by Vaughan Rapatahana. 2011.

Immortelle and bhandaaraa poems, by Lelawattee Manoo-Rahming. 2011.

In vitro, by Laura Solomon. 2nd ed., 2014.

Irreverent Poems for Pretentious People, by Henrik Hoeg, 2016.

Life Lines, by Shahilla Shariff, 2012.

Moving house and other poems from Hong Kong, by Gillian Bickley. 2005.

Of Leaves and Ashes, by Patty Ho, 2016.

Of symbols misused by Mary-Jane Newton. March 2011.

Painting the borrowed house: poems, by Kate Rogers. 2008.

Perceptions. by Gillian Bickley. 2012.

Rain on the Pacific Coast, by Elbert Siu Ping Lee, 2013.

refrain, by Jason S. Polley. 2010.

Shadow play, by James Norcliffe. 2012.

Shadows in Deferment, by Birgit Linder. November 2013.

Shifting Sands, by Deepa Vanjani, 2016.

Sightings, by Gillian Bickley. 2007.

Smoked pearl: poems of Hong Kong and beyond, by Akin Jeje (Akinsola Olufemi Jeje). 2010.

The Layers Between, by Celia Claase, 2015.

Unlocking, by Mary-Jane Newton, 2014.

Wonder, lust & itchy feet, by Sally Dellow. 2011.

POETRY – CHINESE LANGUAGE

For the record and other poems of Hong Kong, by Gillian Bickley. Translated by Simon Chow. 2010. E-bk.

Moving house and other poems from Hong Kong, translated into chinese, with additional material, by Gillian Bickley. Edited by Tony Ming-Tak Yip. Translated by Tony Yip and others. 2008.

~~~

FIND OUT MORE ABOUT OUR AUTHORS BOOKS AND EVENTS

Visit our website:
http://www.proversepublishing.com

Visit our distributor's website:
<www.chineseupress.com>

Follow us on Twitter
Follow news and conversation:
twitter.com/Proversebooks>
OR
Copy and paste the following to your browser window and follow the instructions:
https://twitter.com/#!/ProverseBooks

"Like" us on www.facebook.com/ProversePress

Request our free E-Newsletter
Send your request to info@proversepublishing.com.

Availability
Most books are available in Hong Kong and world-wide from our Hong Kong based Distributor,
The Chinese University Press of Hong Kong,
The Chinese University of Hong Kong, Shatin, NT,
Hong Kong SAR, China.
Email: cup-bus@cuhk.edu.hk
Website: <www.chineseupress.com>.

All titles are available from Proverse Hong Kong
http://www.proversepublishing.com

and the Proverse Hong Kong UK-based Distributor.

We have **stock-holding retailers** in Hong Kong,
Singapore (Select Books),
Canada (Elizabeth Campbell Books),
Andorra (Llibreria La Puça, La Llibreria).
Orders can be made from bookshops in the UK and elsewhere.

Ebooks

Most of our titles are available also as Ebooks.

www.ingramcontent.com/pod-product-compliance
Lightning Source LLC
Chambersburg PA
CBHW071120160426
43196CB00013B/2640